VICTORY IN
GOD

GINGER NOYES ANTOINE

WESTBOW
PRESS®
A DIVISION OF THOMAS NELSON
& ZONDERVAN

WestBow Press books may be ordered through booksellers or by contacting:

WestBow Press
A Division of Thomas Nelson & Zondervan
1663 Liberty Drive
Bloomington, IN 47403
www.westbowpress.com
1 (866) 928-1240

ISBN: 978-1-9736-2184-3 (sc)
ISBN: 978-1-9736-2183-6 (e)

Print information available on the last page.

WestBow Press rev. date: 03/15/2018

T is Glorious to understand that the Bible is spiritually alive. Every word significantly penetrates the heart. I cannot thank God enough for opening the mind to understand scriptures. Each day spent with God is refreshingly soaring, intensity of fearful expectations and comforts in gratifications. My heart cries out in joy because the Spiritual self of me had united in Spirit with his Majesty, the Everlasting Holy Spirit. I remember speaking to a Pastor at Mount Gilead Church. I recalled his name was Shelby. He had told me to read John in the bible, three times. I was quite shocked and questioned as to why? Praise God, that after ten years had gone by; I completely understood why. Because the more that you continued to read, your Soul thirsts and longed for more spiritual food. It is becoming more meditatedly endless. My heart rejoices for the Lord had been so good to me. Heaven and Earth proclaimed Great is the Lord in understanding and marvelous in wisdom.

Through the balcony of the third floor hotel, overlooking the grandeur expanse ocean; my heart praise the Almighty God. O Supreme Glorious Lord, who is exalted forever more over all nations.

The breath of God gives life to every creature. What joyous wonder to see the light of the sun shimmering across the ultraluminating ocean; waves tossing in perfect formation of unification to the sandy seashore, footsteps of seagulls hopping from incoming tides.

How utterly enchanting is the wind blowing softly through rustling palm trees and fragile, tall grass. The spiritual moves ever so in harmony, singing voices of God's commands; seagulls flying swiftly across the sky in perfect, tranquil order. The air is filled with the magnificent Glory of God. How pleasing it is to received this exuberance Spirit of Divine Powers.

2 Peter1:3His divine power has given us everything we need for life and godliness through our knowledge of him who called us by his own glory and goodness. 4Through these he has given us his very great and precious promises, so that through them you may participate in the divine nature and escape the corruption in the world caused by evil desires.

I prayed that every Soul will recognized the momentous Attributes of God's Power living inside their Spirit. Every creation is significantly special in the sight of God, Amen. The eyes of the Lord sees our every imperfections and refining it with each passing day. Each day is glorious because mankind is gifted with every spiritual gifts and can contribute to others in need.

Psalm 91:14"Because he loves me," says the Lord, "I will rescue him; "I will protect him for he acknowledges my Name.

How great is God's love shining on us. Just express to God of your every concerns, the pain that you are going through. The genuiness of a deeply contrite heart is heard by God; allowed God to work in you through the guidance of the Holy Spirit, the Holy Spirit is the integral Spiritual Truths from God(John 16:13-15). The integrity of our heart is considered by God. How we conduct ourselves in life is examined by God to be rewarded in Righteousness of Blessings(Jerem.17:10,1chron.28:9). Where sin is present,consequently;troubles and disciplines will come. Yet the Lord is ever merciful towards mankind in Grace,Generosity of love through Jesus, who gloriously relinquish all authority and power for salvation of souls.

It is a great privilege to surrendered our heart in devotion to God with thanksgiving and prayers. The perseveranced of Humbleness will triumph in victory(Matt.6:9-14). Our acknowledgement of God is Faith in blessing. Faith is complete confidence from fears,deaths,spiritual battles; for the Lord comforted, strengthened, delivered souls in freedom of righteousness.

The physical self in us is a cycle process of change. It is the outer shell of our individuality for purification, transformation to the Spiritual Spirit of God(Romans 8:20-21). Praise God for the Biblical Truths Of Insights to discerned good and evil through the mind.

Ptsd,depressions,suicidal,divorces, drugs and alcohol:

God has the power to cleanse us and to destroy the enemy's assaults. The many strongholds kept the Spirit in prison. We must learn how to detect the movements of deceitfulness. Our heart,prayers,petitions to the Lord must be ultimately strong- confident in belief as well as speaking God's words.

The enemy's assaults is the magnitude of manipulations of the mind through the unconsciousness state. It is introducing fantasies,scenarios,imaginations,lust,excitement,temptations of desires in thoughts,actions;to influence the Spirit within to fear, desires of the flesh,greed,power. Therefore, one must absolutely be alert of the spiritual as well as our interactions with the world and environments.

The main focus is on God,Spiritual Truths, Positivity in all things. Doing good works, contributing to society by making a difference,sports,projects,music,arts- crafts. ***the mind is determined to proceed in a productive, effective task.

***blocked out negative thoughts, for feeding into it will spread like cancer.

Our Spirit is secured if we continued in perseveranced of God's teachings. Church support, family support and spouse, friends who is knowledgeable of the condition, giving space- consideration in establishing a safe, loving, bonding of the home with or without children in peaceful, decent, order environment. Prayers is predominantly powerful to overpowered the enemy, wisdom to all truths; unity of communion with God to become One. Prayed Daily, be healed in power to leadership, duty to countrymen, good works, full of mercy in generosity humility of heart.

Be assured Dear brothers and sisters, for the Lord Almighty is Merciful, Unlimited in Patience, Kindnesses and Abounding in Love. The Lord Almighty's Generosity is beyond measure of Blessings Souls towards Providence Inheritance Freedom to Eternal Peace and Prosperity. All things was greatly considered before the world began(Rev.12:1-17).

The Lord formed all creations within his Spirit; Trust is deeply rooted within self. The creations, image of God; completely protected, disciplined and trained through the Body of Christ(2 Pet.1:3-9,Psalm139:13-16). Every Soul can conquered all (satanic) spiritual battles. Keep in mind, the physical body that we are in, will one day perished; yet the Spirit lives on to God's Eternal Glory. Through many days,hours,months,years; yet much in perseveranced of trials,errors,meditations,biblical studies,prayers,will prevailed in structured, Disciplined Attributes of the Heart of God(Gal.5:22-23).

Beloved, the joy of God is magnificently, spectacularly endured through duty, discipleships of Christ. The cost of the Gospels, there is no price. Faith pursuing in zealous goal in victory; conquering impacts,discomforts,punishments,always faithful encouraging Souls towards Heaven-the Eternal Glory(2 Corin.11:23-33).

Glory be to Almighty God, for every creation is a significant,spiritually gifted Soul. Every day attaining knowledge, wisdom through the core of the Heart of God. The Holy Scriptures are Truths which penetrates Souls in Miracles delivered in Strengths, Character, Power and Glory.

David after God's Heart(1Sam.-2Sam.)

As a young man, David was already trained tending sheeps and dealings with his brothers. The Lord had delivered him from bears and lions (1 Sam.17:37). These many skills had strengthened him to battle against Goliath and the trouble years to come. Predominantly,

Faith was always at the center of David's heart for God; yet the Lord knew that at the heart of every mankind, it is not perfect(gen.3:13-19). The Lord had anointed king Saul, because Israel wanted a king. God's own people did not inquired of God, but to turn towards their own desires(1Sam.8:18). Yet still, God is full of compassion; after David defeated Goliath, he became king Saul's servant, captain of Saul's bodyguard and was highly respected(1Sam.22:14-15).

These passages certainly let it be known to all nations, that the heart can easily be mislead. The love of God is eternally protective always for God's people. David was already predestinated to journeyed for God's purpose. David served king Saul with tremendous heart of loyalties; nevertheless, Saul's jealousy of David was totally destructive until his death at Mount Gilboa (1Sam.18-31).

Tis most tragically horrific in such circumstances, but Praise be to God for giving mankind the privilege to understand the differences between righteousness and unrighteousness of two dynamic men as David and king Saul. The choice is up to the individual, for the rebellious stubborness of the heart is great. God shows the world that the Love of a Holy Father is unchanging, yet discipline must be executed to strengthened and refined the children of God to its ultimate glory.

My heart is in deep agony, for much is within every heart, Everlasting Attributes of God to be victoriously in Joy of comfort; provided in reverenced,honor,praise,thanksgiving to Almighty God. None is greater than the other, One Heart in Body of Christ, a building united to God in Glory before the world began(john17:20-26).

The basis for life is simply Love. Where there is Love, there is giving, forgiveness, protectiveness and abundance in generosity. The glorious generosity love of God ascending to perfection-Grace. Much theological findings is evident through intensive studies of facts and truths of scriptures. The Bible holds wisdom of insights to the spiritual through the life of God's chosen disciples and the coming of Jesus Christ for the Redemption of Souls.

A most benevolence privilege example is Peter healing the crippled beggar(Acts 3:6). A miraculous wonder by the Lord. It wasn't just showing the power of God working, but a devotion to God deeply -always faithful in joyful discipleship of Christ. It is not about materialistic ownerships,positions,or appearances. Divinely, it is the inner beauty, uniqueness quality and humility of heart in action.

Discipleships is enduranced of strength and character,Hope,denying oneself in every way for the benefits of others. Sufferings is persevered to the point of losing one's life; yet joyful for the undying love of Jesus Christ, the giving of everything one has, having little and carrying little, even to mere nothingness(Luke10:3-4). Life is disciplined in great understanding, maturing to glorious children of God.

Everyone has a testimony to share. A woman carrying a child for 9 months before birthing. Raising children-cooking,washing,hanging clothes, cutting grass-home,work,church;caring for the needs of others. Many worked from jobs to jobs; yet still there are those working as farmers-from sun up to sun down, gathering fruits and vegetables by hand.

Have you ever gathered tobacco leaves manually? The sun beating ferociously at you and so is the torturous back pain! Scooping the leaves with your arms in sequence up and down each tobacco row. Once tobacco leaves are gathered, it had to be transferred from a truck to a looper machine. Now workers had to manually gathered tobacco leaves- full of infested insects onto the looper machine as an assembly line; standing all day laying leaves sewn on 2x2x4 to be hung up in a barn for drying. Would anyone now considered A cigarette? Praise the Lord for a cool Coca Cola at break time, a drive to the country store for sandwiches,snacks;after lunch, back to work.

In late summer, dried hung tobacco leaves were taken down and unstrung from 2x2x4 for shipment. Praise be to God when the job is finished, because much cracked sores developed from roughed texture of compositions.

O lord, I am so thankful that those days had gone by and you have given me such a privilege to served,disciplined,shared;open my eyes to experienced life and times of the men and women in uniforms-Always Faithful in Honor,leadership,Duty to countrymen, good works; ever so in trials,testing,deployments,self denying, unimaginable bloodshed. So many youths, brave men of all walks of life. Many reminded me of my children, young- grown to serve in life. Yes, my heart goes out to them deploying to war, heavy duffel bags, tired physique, weight loss; vivid lines, sunken eyes of prolonged sleep deprivation exhaustion. Tis joyful to see them chatting anxiously leaving base and getting supplies. Taxis rushing through roads and highways like a speeding contest. Their vehicles is like changing tires. They too must work to provide for their families just like everybody else.

How much so, one labored in life. the scriptures specifically mentioned about Adam and Eve(Gen.3:16-24). Through all things, unified in developing a great splendorous purpose to God's Glory.

Every Soul is a leader, gloriously designed by our Creator. In this life, many things shall come to pass. As examplified biblically, leadership requires trials,tests,disciplinary actions and consequently; according to God's Will(2Sam.5:1-5). We cannot avoided it,because this world that we live in is of the Spiritual Battle of the World. Great are troubles and temptations to overcome. King David, himself was evidently faced with the situation of Bathsheba and Uriah. No matter how strong one considered himself to be, the mind is so easily influenced to sin(2Sam.11). The great impacts of downfalls is extremely destructive. It destroys lives in so many ways; yet changing the pattern of our lives according to God's will and purposes.

How humbled should the heart become so. A heart that is deeply contrite, will be of much godly sorrow towards righteousness over wrongs. The focal point is to do good and of mercy towards all men. Because the heart of the individual is open to the understanding of how to forgive and acknowledges the selfishness and desires within self. This glorious new spiritual part of man is absolutely blessed with the Eternal Light of God manifested within his Spirit.

And that is why David could be so giving towards his countrymen. Sinning against God is a matter of Retribution. Not one Soul is without sin! There is always the consequences of sins; for much troubles continues to be fallen David. The agonizing death of his infant son with Bathsheba. The child died from illness. Yet still David had to endured the opposition of Absalom, his very own son; who is after his life. How tragic is the circumstances of Amnon raping Tamar; sister of both Amnon and Absalom(2Sam.13).

Troubles on top of troubles came to David. Throughout much of his life, David's household were full of disastrous events as prophesyed by Nathan from the Lord(2Sam.12). How fearful should one be at the hands of the Almighty God? Upon careful examinations of our journey in life, we absolutely can recognizes every discipline, errors. Our lives is ultimately at the Mercy of the Lord; Thanksgiving in Humility Healed by the Power of his Grace! The Purity Generosity Love of God strengthened our Spirit to act of much consideration towards mankind's sufferings(Hebrews13:3). What a spectacular lesson to be learned; a blessing of such knowledge, for it could be profoundedly a worse scenario facing our judgement.

After the tragic horrific death of Absalom at the hands of Joab- David's commander; David returns to Jerusalem. (2 Sam.19:14)He won over the hearts of all the men of Judah as though they were One man. They sent word to the king,return,you and all your men.

Great is the humility of heart, fulfilled Attributes of God-the Fruit of the Spirit restored Israel in Peace. Whether young or old, high positions, low born, poorest of the poor and even those that done wrong; David gave and shared all that he has as well as showing them pardons.

This Generosity, Humbleness of Spirit, extended to countrymen in all Purity of Love. David understood the Love of God for the Unity of Mankind to become Oneness with God. Through much brokenness and bloodshed, David knew that even though such is the responsibility; children of God must be considered in Justice and Righteousness. The physical self transformed to the spiritual realm to give Honor,Praise,Glory and Thanksgiving to God. David was a man after God's Heart. The Lord made him a Lamp in Jerusalem, because he did what God tells him to do. As mention by the Apostle Paul, David was the Prophet of God(1Kings15:3-5,Acts 13:22,Acts2:30).

O Lord, Great is your Love of Blessings to be Knowledgeable and Honored your Name. Every Soul is divinely blessed to all understanding and disciplined to become the glorious children of God. The miraculous wonders of your love continues with every passing day. Amen.

EQUALITY

Today, we lived in a very critical, catastrophic times. The world is changing in so many differences of approach. Let us together prayed and remembered the teachings of God so that Our heart may be united in joyful comfort of glory.

Exodus1:8 Then a new king, who did not know about Joseph, came to power in Egypt.9 "Look, "he said to his people, "the Israelites have become much too numerous for us(Exodus1:9:22).

This new king feared that the expansion, fruitful growth of the Israelites would become confidently independent from the control of Egypt. So then, the Israelites were oppressed with forced labor. Great is the compassion, mercy of God, the birthing of Moses came to be. Moses destiny was to lead God's people to freedom; miraculous wonders of deliverenced through the desert of the Jordan. God's own people rebelled against God in distrust(Deut.1:26-46).

What a devastation when children do not respect the unconditional love given. Love foresees in all splendorous, generosity before the world began.

Deut.28:20The Lord will send on you curses, confusion and rebuke in everything you put your hand to, until you are destroyed and come to sudden ruin because of the evil you have done in forsaking him.

It is a fearful expectation of God's wrath for disobedience. O Lord, Thanksgiving for your Everlasting Eternal Love to open the eyes in all wisdom and understanding, hope towards joy and peace.

And so is the destruction of Jerusalem being prophesyed by Jeremiah; the invasion of Nebuchadnezza,king of Babylon occurred in desolation(Jerem.32:26-44). Yet the Lord always Faithful in doing good for mankind because of his great compassion. God's promise of restoration for Judah, Israel and Jerusalem continues in prosperity. The lands were healed in purification through the Love of God's forgiveness.

Jerem.33:15" In those days and at that time I will make a righteous branch sprout from David's line; he will do what is just and right in the land.

Through the course of biblical history; the Lord had reached out towards mankind numerously. What proclamations and miracles of wonders. Such is the deliverance towards healing in righteousness.

Should the Covenant between God and Man be broken? If so, will nations suffered at the hands of the God Almighty(Jerem.34:13-22)?

All Truths is evident according to scriptures within the passages of the book Jeremiah. God declares freedom of righteousness for all mankind. All Men Are Created Equal. Those that continues to forsakes God's proclamations will be proclaim in fearful wrath of judgement and destructions. The Lord is in Full Control of the Order of the World. Nothing goes unnoticed before him. All unrighteousness of every nation is seen by the eyes of God. The course and destiny is within God's Great Purpose. Disobedience and the sheer evilness stubborness continuance will results in much consequences. Wars,plague,famine and catastrophic forces in nature are resulted from the condemnation judgement of God.

Jerem.27:5With my great power and outstretched arm I made the earth and its people and the animals that are on it, and I give it to anyone I please. 6 Now I will hand all your countries over to my servant Nebuchadnezzar king of Babylon; I will make even the wild animals subject to him. 7 All nations will serve him and his grandson until the time for this land comes; then many nations and great kings will subjugate him.

All things had certainly came to pass. The life of every heart will be determined at the set time, places and events. Are not the Will of God set in motion? How much so are mankind trembling before the Almighty God. The earth and all nations created are at the mercy of the Living God. God had spoken through God's chosen servants of the disciplinary actions. Nothing that does evil goes without punishment. For the justice of God triumphs in righteousness.

How often does one faced troublesome circumstances in life? It is the choice that was committed to, troubles on top of troubles. However, the Lord is magnificent in heart of generosity for the purification of Souls to

Eternal Inheritance of Life(1Kings2:2-4). Therefore, the Spirit within us must watch and pray so that it will not be weakened by the world. Because Faith living within is strength and discernment of right and wrong. Each day with God gives great joy of spiritual blessings as the rising of the sun,seasons,day and night. The Lord had set everything in motion for the glorious perfection road of redemption. Jesus, the Son of God, heals all wounds to God's Eternal Light.

The Lord does not desired to destroy mankind as in the days of Noah. But had always instructed with much care and consideration, disciplined in the hope for Souls to become the glorious image of God himself. Where Love is the declaration of truth, wisdom and freedom. Our tears will be replaced and refreshed in joyous singing.

The Lord had shown humanity that it isn't about how a person's appearance is, but it is the love in action of unity to the pursuit of happiness. The Kingdom of God is within, a Divine Holy Temple. The Crucifixion of Jesus Christ pierced our heart and shattered all strongholds; uniting with God in guidances of the Holy Spirit. Souls are the divine new creation in Christ. Praise God for the endured, perseverance consummation of the Body of Christ.

If one gives freely in every way to the needs of other, joy had bloomed in exultation of glory. In order to understand God so explicitly, seek God daily wholeheartedly. The Spirit within surrendered in hearing God's Words with open willingness,believe,Confessing,repented,baptized through the death, burial and resurrection of Christ in faithfulness. For the Body of Christ, a unified saints of God knitted together like Angels in Heaven Worshipping God(John2:17Psalm69:9). Though the testing of times is of trying endurances, the Will of God surpasses all things. By trusting in God completely, the enemy's attack is futile, ineffectual. For the Divine Powers of God strengthened and delivered in Victory. As the heart grows in fervor of God, there is only Honor, Praise, Glory, thanksgiving in reverence to God.

*GOD IN ACTION

Upon much meditation of Faith in seeking God, great are the revelations of scriptures. The life and time of Hezekiah, king of Judah and Sennacherib, king of Assyria, gives an immensity revelation that God is the One and Only True God, in Power and Glory.

2kings18:11 The king of Assyria deported Israel to Assyria and settleled them in Halah, in Gozan on the Habor River and in towns of the Medes.12 This happened because they had not obeyed the Lord their God, but had violated his covenant- all that Moses the servant of the Lord commanded. They neither listened to the commands nor carried them out.

It is of total destructive consequences for disobedience to God, because without the support of God; the Assyrians took over Samaria. Sennacherib,king of Assyria, was full of pride and confidence of his own beliefs as well as the conquests cities of Judah. Sennacherib incited,challenged,threatened Jerusalem, sending words against the Almighty God which led to his downfall in condemnation.

2kings 18:35 Who of all gods of these countries has been able to save his land from me? How then can the lord deliver Jerusalem from my hand?

Now when Hezekiah king of Judah heard this, he inquired of the lord through Isaiah. The Lord was with him daily in successful battles. Isaiah sent message to Hezekiah through his officials concerning the king of Assyria.

*2kings19:7 Listen! I am going to put such a Spirit in him that when he hears a certain report, he will return to his own country, and there I will have him cut down with the sword(2kings19:35-37).

The Lord is True to his Words. For every man's life is at the hands of Almighty God.

Thanksgiving Lord, for shaping and molding me. My heart rejoiced for through your disciplined and training; the results laid open before my eyes to see changes,transformation,great is your mercy in the course of my life and patterns of strengths, character developing in me as well as my children. Thank you Lord for confidence of your love unchanging, living within my Spirit. You, O Lord hears my pain,sorrows,weaknesses,tears,singing in humility to your rewarding teachings and wisdom to prosperity. The spiritual part of me knows that I am not alone, for you have been with me- forming me within your Spirit. I am strong in Oneness with his Majesty-the Everlasting Eternal God. My life is not my own any more. Magnificent Lord, the fearful wrath of you had open my eyes to see the world in humbleness of heart and joy! Glory be to your Name, Almighty God! Hallelujah!!!

O My Lord and Savior, I recalled so many days,fears,failures consumed my Soul. The Negativity controlled and weighed me down to its domineering thoughts,Criticisms,yet Faithful is your Love always guiding me because I surrendered all in confession. Praise be to you O Lord, for I repented of my sins through your death, burial and resurrection. Great is confidence of you embracing my soul. My heart rejoices,prayed,singing,cried wholeheartedly in thanksgiving to your Holy Name.

Who or what am I, unworthy servant, my Lord-that you should considered in making all things possible? The Last Supper, reproduction from Leonardo, completed within 4 months. My eyes so severed dried, yet you guided my hands to mix and paint colors in tears of your Love, Grace and Mercy through every lines, brushings. How endless days your words cuts through my heart in writings, desperately searching every depth and corners to know You,O Lord, and Faith of Hope for the creations abounding inheritance of Glory.

Deut.30:14No,the word is very near you; it is in your mouth and in your heart so you may obey it.15See,I set before you today life and prosperity, death and destruction.16For I command you today to love the Lord your God, to walk in his ways, and to keep his commands, decrees and laws; then you will live and increase, and the Lord your God will bless you in the land you are entering to possess.

Thanksgiving O Lord, my heart, my Soul, my Spirit, my joy, my strength, my mind, my comfort. Every blessings is within every Soul, significantly in generosity of your abundance glorious characteristics,O Lord-giving sustanance,strengths and gratifications. All negatives can turn to positive, downfalls and disappointments declines in unproductive exhaustion, yet victoriously prosperous through the unlimited patience, and goodness of you O Lord throughout the generations.

Hosea4:6My people are destroyed from lack of knowledge. "Because you have rejected knowledge, I also reject you as my priests; because you have ignored the law of your God, I also will ignore your children.

And because great is unconditional love of consideration, perseverance of disciplinary actions overcomes weaknesses triumphantly. In order to become Holy, the Spirit is refined. And to be refined, the Spirit absolutely goes through unveiling of all impurities. This simply means getting rid of sins. Rebuked it in the Name of Jesus; stand firm and determined in wholehearted unison with God. Let no one change your path, towards righteousness. If you find yourself in the hopelessness state of being, speak sincerely to God with all your heart and soul of complete confession, integrity of humility. Your voice is of a deeply contrite heart that will be heard, pleasing in the sight of God;sing,cried,prayed,read and meditate God's words daily, for great are divine blessings of joy within-waiting to be unveiled! There is no more fears because we are the solid rock; the immovable foundation that cannot be broken!

Remember always to Praise,Honor,Glorified and Thanksgiving to God, for all good things comes from Eternal God. *Give to the Lord what you Love the Most-Denying Habits Leading to Death, even if it may seem difficult, impossible, heart wrenching; the mercy and divine powers of God is all powerful in complete effectiveness to make your burdens light and healed in exultation, purity, holiness.

Hosea3:1The Lord said to me, "go, show your love to your wife again, though she is loved by another and is an adulteress. Love her as the Lord loves the Israelites, though they turn to other gods and love the sacred raisin cakes.

O Divine Holy Father God, Complete Faithfulness, Generosity beyond measure in Forgiveness so that the creations be unified to Eternal glory. Such splendors gloriously blessed in seasons, day and night, raindrops nourishing the earth in joyous singing. The Road to Salvation bloomed in rays of Love soaring, astoundingly, richly, immeasurably of kindnesses and to experiences a profoundly unconditional spiritual realm of deliverance liberated from all iniquities to the Everlasting Freedom of Righteousness(Luke4:1-13).

*** Bewared,the destructive forces of darkness weakens the world with the manipulations for power and control which only leads to the enslavement of eternal fire!

*** Behold in Confidence! The Lamb of God, Risen Christ, keeps Eternal Sons of God through Baptismal of Faith. Victory is within, Lighting all those in Christ to be quickened to God. Peace given Generously, totally committed in all faithfulness of justice. (Ephe.2:14-18,Romans8:10-17).

Fruitful Rewards:

THREE SIGNIFICANT MEDITATIONS

(1) Examined the integrityness of the heart-recognized strengths and weaknesses.

(2) The conscience of the heart must make a decision based upon facts,evidence,knowledge.

(3) If the intent of actions are dishonest,gained;certainly the heart will encountered a sinking revelation of fear,guilt,shameful complex. The Spirit is hampered and imprisoned within Satan's stronghold in the intensity influences of destructive temptations.

***The sincerity heart of a child of God must lay bare open before the Lord; prayed wholeheartedly of mind, strength and Soul.

***Triumphantly, one should considered in any given situation-

(A) Is this right?

(B) Are the focal points just?

(C) Is the resolution fair?

These three components are positively beneficial in blessings of fruitful freedom of righteousness and because predominantly, a joyous giving in heart which transcends wisdom,understanding,knowledge,and imminently the course of direction in life. No longer are Souls in bondage of Satan, but to be set free from the fearful wrath judgement of God to the Eternal Joy of Glory.

How much so is the heart in the completeness of Trusting for Truth and being disciplined for deliverance of sins to the acknowledgement that God is the One and Only True God! what joyous of Blessings in complete Unity, Generosity immeasurably Bestowed upon the creations before the world began.(john17:20-26)

Praise You, O Lord; for you knew me before I was formed in my mother's womb. My Lord you rescued me from a land of wars and turmoil; changing the course of my life to a promised providence of joy. There are not enough words to Thank you for the generosity of your merciful Plans of the heart.

Through much trials of marriage, raising three outstandingly challenging children; the privilege to cared for a most beautiful child, that had been to six homes,divorce;yet,so much more than I could ever envision.

O Lord, when I was just a young babe in Christ, you taught me how to pray. I felt a calling to visit the elderly in nursing homes. How frightful I felt, yet something kept leading me there. I did not know how to pray, but to just say," hello, my name is Ginger, may I pray for you". Thanksgiving Lord, for Faith in you guided me to hold the fragile hands and say," I love you". Days,weeks,months went by; it was much easier. My heart rejoices, twas amazingly wonderful to see the glittering, tired eyes lighted up, gentle smiles and yet such desperation of urgency among souls.

Something,touchingly,inexpressively,exuberantly moving within my Spirit to expand; to focused on the plan of salvation, to share with everyone that I came in contact with. Young or old; no matter who you are, my heart opens up to share about the good news. I even started doing it in the water. Great are the dangers of my inexperience. So much are the temptations came one by one. So much changes is taking place, people, events came my way.

I started praying more so and decided to collect money for the missionaries. Have never done anything like this in my whole life, don't know where to begin. Right before Christmas, I went to the Mall with a large envelope. Upon entering; an elderly lady with her husband were watching singing bears, quickly I asked her, "excuse me mam, would you like to donate one dollar to the missionary?" Immediately, she wheeled her husband away. I was stricken with shock; yet I continued on. A gentleman was in my view, I then also asked him; much to my dismayed, he gave me a look of disbelief! Sadly, I walked toward Sears and approached a young cashier. "Hi, would you like to donate one dollar for the missionaries?" I said. She answered," I have a sandwich, "would you like it?" "O no, thank you," I said. Embarrassed, I walked away. Then, I saw a Police Officer and quickly walked away. Next, I came to a shoe shop. I asked the salesman for the donation, "get a letter from the institution or churches and we can go from there, "he replied. I thanked him and was hopeful. Upon leaving the Mall; I came across the same man that was sitting down earlier, he gave me three dollars. Joyfully, I thanked him. He told me that he thought I was for real about missionaries. Excitedly, I invited him to church.

Following the week, I went to church and asked for a letter of recommendations and was denied, great is my heart in total devastation! I approached families and friends, some gave; yet many looked at me with much distrusts and thought I was completely insane. Several weeks went by, I walked throughout the flea market asking for donations; receiving unbelievable looks, still some responded.

Nevertheless, I was able to collect over $70.00 and placed it in the missionary box. The sum were few, yet what joy to my heart. Tis a great lesson to be learned. I now can see how it is for the homeless.

Life is certainly a journey of challenges, lessons to explore, expand; a Hope for Truths!

Yes, for quite some years, working odds and ends jobs, cashiers, ;when the children were small; whether cutting grass on week-ends, I humbly thanked the Lord for he was with me every step of the way, keeping me strong.

I remembered, a most interestingly lady of character; named, Mary McDewelle, Professional Artist, intellectual, compassionate in life, people, loves the Lord, great joy of love for her excitedly companion-chuwawah, Peewee. A Lady of Noble Character as well as uniquely disciplined, disabled condition, much to be observed. You can learn so much from her; independent way of living.

Quite some years back, met a wholesome couple, Rick, Renee Harward and their awesomely four sons-Dusty, Micah, Alex and Kendrick; great was their wholehearted love in taking many children to the church with them. My two young, strong- minded siblings, Chris, Dominique, was full of joy. Spent many days playing with rabbits and going to churches activities. Then during the next several years, much Biblical guidance with Pastor John and Dottie Pabon. This was a great exploration for growth of fellowships, interactions among youths, Biblical studies, plays which promotes positivity for them as well as overcoming challenges. My oldest, Brian, always more matured beyond his age; diligence in studies, jobs, Praise the Lord.

No matter what are the circumstances in the children's nurturing years; they knew that their education was important! Always on a daily basis; they were reprimanded in doing home works-reading, writing, mathematics. Thanksgiving to the Lord for guiding their footsteps. Twas not easy with working. Through the brokenness of marriage, changes their life. They are more independent, angry, resentful. Heartbreakingly as it is; time, maturing, the love of God is healing, forgiveness.

Children are extremely intelligent, it is the wholesome, wholeheartedness of your love, bonding in blessings of joy through the Fruit of the Spirit. During much of my trials and afflictions, I attended the Church of Christ at Village Drive and Country Club. Though weighed down in depression, many days felt like I was not going to make it; yet Faith in God kept me going. Never have I heard so many scriptures in my life! The truth will set you free! How true, because the Words of God takes action, penetrates into your heart! Do not let anyone take away your Hope or degraded you in any way, for God's Words stands; giving wisdom, and understanding of revelations. No matter what the circumstances you find yourself in, the integrityness of your heart in complete surrendering to God, for Great is his Mercy in making all things possible. Praise God for carrying my burdens. My

Heart and Soul was zealous in seeking God, to know everything about God. Now after ten years, Thanksgiving to the Lord for Restoration. O lord how magnificent is your love, the Body of Christ, Compassionate in every way to do good so that Souls unconditionally Love you Faithfully in Obedience! My heart rejoices in your Words, confidence living within me to do all things. I am strong because your compassion is like no other! Joy had lifted me up in singing to glorified your Holy Name. Love filled deeply within my Soul to make positive changes, to Repent, to forgive others; generosity in all humbleness.

Marriage is of deep love and respect. A Devotion to God in prayers, worship, coming together as One Body, One Church, Christ, God as the head over all. The brokenness, failures occurred because there is no consistency of deep love and respect. Love must be grounded in complete consideration-sharing chores, tasks. Youths and beauty fades over the years, but much is the nurturing, cares for the well being of each other, Soul, Spirit and Body. It cannot be one-sided, always working together sharing ideas, common goals, pushing forward for the betterment of the Body. The Generosity of heart to know what are the weaknesses and strengthened each other towards success. As a Body- family, set boundaries, understand the teachings of God, not only at church only, but at home as well, uniting and building up faith, knowledge, avoiding the influential of the worldly.

You cannot change the past, but to move forward in all positivity. Being a mother, I humbly shared with my children the love, deep contriteness when I am wrong, tell them that I am sorry, I am not perfect; letting them see my love through wet, cold, rainy, sunny days, whether getting them to school, watching, waiting for many days gone by already becoming young men and woman. Through much perseverance, prayed, never give up; Restoration in God gives Joy. Today, Love had bloomed so ever more among my children and grandchildren. I had learned to let go too, because children grows up and have a mind of their own. I will always be supportive, counsel and let them know Truths. They have dreams, goals and partners to shared in life. The Lord has been with me throughout my trials; carrying me every step of the way. My heart rejoices in thankfulness to my Savior, for the children are so Blessed in many ways. Confidently in Faith is, "Do my best and God will do the rest". Amen.

Truthfully, I may have been dead a few times, but the Lord was my cushion, sun and shield; protecting me from enemy's assaults. No matter what you have experienced, seen, done; be strong, listen not to the thoughts of suicidal or allowed anyone to put you down. Walked away from unwanted remarks! If it endangered your life, let it be known. Always remember that you are a special child of God! If you are in the wrong, prayed for the person that you have wronged and above all, forgive others for offenses because strongholds, sins, becoming evil dominion of control, destructive. Forgiveness is releasing impurities, burdens.

Acts15:8 God, who knows the heart, showed that he accepted them by giving the Holy Spirit to them, just as he did to us. 9 He made them no distinction between us and them, for he purified their hearts by faith.

The Lord had shown the world that we are One people. We breathe, shared great physical essential needs, not one is greater than the other. My Soul Praises, Honor, Reverence and Thanksgiving to the Lord in holiness for all that he has done. I looked deeply within the heart of every Soul, seeing the uniqueness, kindness, beauty of the inner self; not degrading anyone, but prayed for them to be blessed with joy, Amen.

Acts14:16 In the past, he let all nations go their own way. 17 Yet he has not left himself without testimony: he has shown kindness by giving you rain from heaven and crops in their seasons; he provides you with plenty of food and fills your hearts with joy.

The splendor of the earth is full of God's Glory. All is open for the eyes to see! The goodness of God is so ever present and generously given within every Soul to live a life of joy, prosperity; peace and equality. Is it not the rebellious nature of sin that one chooses that destroyed the Everlasting Crown given by our Eternal Father God?

Deut.8:17 You may say to yourself," my power and the strength of my hands have produced this wealth for me." 18 But remember the Lord your God, for it is he who gives you the ability to produce wealth and so confirms his covenant, which he swore to your forefathers, as it is today. 19 If you ever forget the Lord your God and follow other gods and worship and bow down to them, I testify against you today that you will surely be destroyed. Like the nations the Lord destroyed before you, so you will be destroyed for not obeying the Lord your God.

Let every Soul rejoices in Peace of God which strengthened, comforted and healed all wounds. No longer will the creations be in bondage, dying decayed; but to be set free through repentance of faith. Thanksgiving to the Lord for his Words is Wisdom. There is no confusion or hopelessness; but God-Fearing Reverence Crown of Grace. Time after time, the Lord is so ever giving humanity his unlimited patience towards purification, justification of Eternal Life. One must understand that the heart should be of utmost sincerity before the Lord. All things will come in unity for those who stands firm, grounded, persevered for Truth. Can we not see the righteousness of God throughout his miraculous wonders? The teachings of God had always been of positivity of doing good.

Acts 10:34 Then Peter began to speak: " I now realize how true it is that God does not show favoritism 35 but accepts men from every nation who fear him and do what is right.

Much had occurred in the city of Joppa. Many were healed and brought to the understanding of Jesus Christ. The magnificent generosity Love of God blesses Jews, gentiles through faith. Tis a great lesson of Peter and Cornelius interactions with each other; for God made it possible for the forgiveness of sins. The Lord looks at our heart and sees into every motives, deeds, prayers. If we are faithful in doing good and helping the poor; how much greater is the reward, for love expressing through actions, prayers and petitions.

The Lord Jesus had taught the disciples expressively of caring for each other through the washing of their feet before his betrayal. (John13:1-17)

*O lord, beloved Son of God, always faithful, gloriously humbled himself so that the creations may understand completely the joy of Love in Equality-that is created beings in uniformity, fairness and justice. *Together may we shed tears, for Equality defines that every Soul are related; a Spiritual Body connected to the Lord. Humanity are Eternally Blessed, Amen. Praise, Glory and Honor be to the Lord.

Let us proclaim the joy within our heart in Eternal singing gladness of tidings!

Jerem.32:41I will make an Everlasting Covenant with them: I will never stop doing good to them, and I will inspire them to fear me, so that they will never turn away from me. 41 I will rejoice in doing them good and will assuredly plant them in this land with all my heart and soul.

And so how true is the Lord shown the world through the Fall of Jerusalem, Gedaliah Assassination and flight to Egypt. (Jerem.39-44)

Tis a most critical, heart wrenching revelation that faith is the ultimate divine powers of God in recognitive truths to inner Peace!

The love of God is revered in exultation! Believe wholeheartedly by surrendering total self, desires, failures in the acceptance of heart, soul and body towards communion with God. Every blessings is within humanity. The Lord is so gracious throughout the generations; making every miraculous wonders in rescuing the creations towards the path of Eternal Deliverance of Righteousness.

*How much so was the Lord's compassion to delivered his people from Egypt; aliens whom the Lord so loved from slavery? Yet, this Generosity of Love was dishonored in returning to Egypt again after the Fall of Jerusalem.

*Jerem.34:17 "Therefore, this is what the Lord says: you have not obeyed me; you have not proclaimed freedom for your fellow countrymen. So I now proclaim 'freedom' for you, declares the Lord-freedom to fall by the sword, plague and famine. I will make you abhorrent to all the kingdoms of the earth.

This is a most Disciplined Lesson in history! There is the ultimate price to pay for disobedience. The Mercy of the Lord is great, may the humility of a humble heart accepted all consequences in Hope of Glory, in Jesus Name, Amen. Because the Lord first loved us, should we not also love as the lord?

Thanksgiving Lord, for your good Spirit was for mankind to be like you in every way. O Lord, how magnificently in holiness, purity of heart you are. The Beloved Jesus Christ, Son of God, endured all sins for deliverance of Souls to Spiritual Eternal Glory.

The Lord Jesus ultimately is glorified by ascending to Heaven so that Souls would be empowered with the shimmering light fusion of the Holy Spirit which transcends all understanding of God! Hallelujah! Amen!

*O Lord, be glorified, how much greater is it for mankind to love each other with all Heart and Soul, doing which is good in Freedom of Justice and Equality; for all differences can be resolved. The joy of the Lord is within every Soul for direction, instruction and rebuking encouragingly disciplined commitment of trustworthiness.

Honored Holy Father God, thank you, thank you; Souls stand up in Victory, embraced the illuminated glorious Spiritual Eternal Enlightenment of your Glory, in Jesus Name, Amen.

O what Joy, for at the heart of God, there is only Supremacy Grace of Truth. Our Heavenly,Marvelous, Wonderful Father, unconditionally Blessed the Creations with Everlasting Life splendidly molded in exquisitely radiant Light. This Magnificent Light sparkles in Immortal Brilliance, Unison of Glory; astoundingly, comfortingly abounding in complete Truths.

2Corin.8:9For you know the Grace of our Lord Jesus Christ, that though he was rich, yet for your sakes, he became poor, so that you, through his poverty might become rich.

The path of righteousness is an outpouring,wholeheartedness loyalty in giving. The magnitude sincerity of love must be demonstrated no matter what the price may be. How so can one truly love with such intensity? The Lord Jesus undergo all sufferings, so that Souls would be splendidly fruitful, prolific; morally and spiritually excellent with God in holiness.

*2Corin.8:14At the present time your plenty will supply what they need; so that in turn their plenty will supply what you need. Then there will be equality,15as it is written: "he who gathered much did not have too much, and he who gathered little did not have too little."

Thanksgiving Lord, for you gave since the beginning of the creations of the world. The Glory of your Love shines throughout the universe, blessing all humanity an Abundance in Prosperity Everlasting.

*** Guilt complex in fruitful joy of glory:

*** Faith in God. The negative can turn to positive!

Trials/	fears/	afflictions/
Interrupter/	desires/	anger/
	Flesh/	

*Overcoming the negative will required one to be of complete dedication, faithfulness, supplication of Oneness to the Spirit of God.

1John5:19We know that we are children of God, and that the whole world is under the control of the evil one.20We know also that the Son of God has come and has given us understanding, so that we may know him who is true. And we are in him who is true---even in his Son Jesus Christ. He is the true God and eternal life.

The Evil One introduces scenarios of pasts, places, events, friends, enemies, illusions, fantasies, desires; dreams that initiates, creates the emotions of influence within its Demonic dominion and control, wills and purposes.

FAITH IN GOD

*(1)Believe

*(2)The gospel plan of salvation:

Hear,believe,repent,confess,baptized,faithful

*(3)Be strong

*(4)Prayed daily

*(5)Thanksgiving to the Lord for what he has done for you.

*(6)Confesses wholeheartedly of all trials, afflictions that is troubling you.(sins)

*(7)Sing,cried,let the Lord sees your complete submission, openness of heart.

Healing begins with the Confession of Sins. Much sufferings must be let go, so that the Lord can carried the burdens for you.

***(8)Give Glory to God-prayers, good deeds, duty, countrymen, godliness, integrity, faithfulness in Honoring God.

***John19:11Jesus answered, "you would have no power over me if it were not given to you from above. Therefore the one who handed me over to you is guilty of a greater sin."(*12-16)

*Psalm2:10Therefore,you kings, be wise; be warned, you rulers of the earth.11Serve the Lord with fear and rejoice with trembling.

* Beloved, there is no One like the Lord Jesus! Faithful and True so that the Gospel would be fulfilled! This is a most glorious point in history examplified for all generations to understand the depth and height of God's Love. The revelation of great leadership is much to be understood. authority that is given, must be executed in all faithfulness. The many roles, positions-soldiers, faces oppositions, duty, commands-disciplined; yet triumphantly, confidently, pardoned through the merciful, Goodness of God himself. Biblical evidence is written in all Truths, revealing confidence, Eternal Hope of Glory. Amen.

COMPLETE CONFIDENCE

Isaiah 61:6"For I, the Lord, love justice; I hate robbery and iniquity. In my faithfulness I will reward them and make an everlasting covenant with them.

Isaiah 61:11For as the soil makes the sprout come up and a garden causes seeds to grow, so the Sovereign Lord will make righteousness and praise spring up before all nations.

Great are blessings enriched the Heaven and Earth. What astoundingly richness of Grace and Mercy. How enchantingly, joyful excitement, like floating endlessly-flying softly; faster and faster, rising across the clear blue sky in freedom's Everlasting!

One early spring, tis joy in my heart to see buds blooming among trees, shrubs, open fields and meadows. I thanked the Lord for the breath of life lifted me up gloriously these many years! As a child, I did not know his Majesty, but just drifted away in my waywardness; yet the Lord was always there guiding me patiently. Rebelliously I made a choice of my own freewill. Trials and tribulations engulfed my life; what a disciplined life endured. Yes, great are testings came my way; Satan had sifted me as wheat, Praise be to the Lord, I am strong because of his Mercy.

In the midst of my iniquities, I came to the Church of Christ, heavy burden of my Soul; wholeheartedly seeking, searching daily, questioning all things. Days, months, years; O my Oil of Joy, thank you, thank you, you healed me and give me Hope. O Lord, you opened my heart to be humbled, for I trusted, believe in your Words. I surrendered my Spirit to you in Confessions. Praise you O Lord for disciplined me in perseveranced of humility to understand the death, burial and resurrection- gift of Eternal Life Everlasting.(1John5:11-12)

Circumstances and all that I came in contact with, shaped and molded me because of the Generosity Providence of Glory. Love in contriteness filled my heart to see that Souls are all the parts coming together to become One with God! There is only a consuming outpouring Divine Love, all things is meaningless; what matters is Forgiveness, peace.

Today, tomorrow, great are blessings! The Lord is Good! Though winter is here, rain fell and nourishes the Earth. A cold wind blows so ever, brown-golden leaves falls softly, gently across the front yard. Many white pansies planted across the fence; season changes, gracefully, cheerfully, fluttering-gently in joyous singing. Wild flowers grew among the front steps of the house, miraculously sprouting here and there. Palm trees swaying, still, quietly, embracing the air, raindrops ever so; surprisingly, knockout roses blooms gloriously in full view for all to see. Only Magnificent God could do such wonders of joy. Amen.

O Lord, how thankful for another year. This year, you blessed a little garden filled with fresh cabbage, yellow squash, buckets full of green peppers. Praise you O Lord, for teaching us to not waste so; you supplied us just enough for nourishment! Many days, you've given us rest within your spacious house in peace, joy and comforts. Thanksgiving Lord, in Jesus name, Amen.

O Lord, each morning you woke me up out of slumber; my heart rejoices. I remember days gone by, racing speedily with times, events;

listen not to your wonderful counseling and great wisdom. *Tears filled my eyes, for you formed me within your Spirit, patiently waiting for me to willingly, lovingly surrendered all to you wholeheartedly in heart, soul, mind and Spirit. How blessed I am. I see your love throughout the universe Lord. Every churches singing Praises to your Name. All that I bring as offerings to you, all came from you. Amen, Amen. Thanksgiving to the Lord, God Almighty!

Majesty of my heart, how can I, a lowly, humbled Spirit could ever be of consideration? You,O Lord, Gloriously, Unlimitedly, Eternally, Generously; full of mercy and goodness!

*1Thes.4:16For the Lord himself will come down from Heaven, with a loud command, with the voice of the archangel and with the trumpet call of God, and the dead in Christ will rise first.17After that, we who are still alive and are left will be caught up together with them in the clouds to meet the Lord in the air. And so we will be with the Lord forever.18Therefore encourage each other with these words.

*Rev.20:13The sea gave up the dead that were in it, and death and hades gave up the dead that were in them, and each person was judged according to what he had done.14Then death and hades were thrown into the lake of fire. The lake of fire is the second death.15If anyone's name was not found written in the book of life, he was thrown into the lake of fire.

*Fear God and do right! The first death is physical death, the second death is spiritual death.

Rev.3:21to him who overcomes, I will give the right to sit with me on my throne, just as I overcame and sat down with my father on his throne.22He who has an ear, let him hear what the spirit says to the churches.

The Plans of the Lord is so ever laid open before mankind to see; guiding with every step so that children of God should be completely confident, thus, may overcoming evil in disciplined, perseveranced, obedienced Will of God.

Praise be to the Lord, for giving the unworthy servant the privilege to worship him in Spirit and Truth. The Lord was gracious, merciful, beyond all things, in making the writings possible. During the first book written, massive itchy, ugly sores broke out throughout my body; was hospitalized for four days. Prayed in desperation for relief; the doctors finally reached to the conclusion-fungal infection and was treated right away. Thanksgiving Lord, for answering my plead. My heart rejoices and attended church the following Wednesday night after leaving the hospital. Thanksgiving to the Lord. Amen. Much interruptions of calls and surprising visits came there after; dismayed, receiving hospital bills one after another. Then the writings of the second book; severed eye infection and painful hip injury to a fall.

Yet, I continued to write, study, frustrated throughout the night, searching, meditating scriptures upon scriptures, meanings, battling dryed eyes; many days struggling in libraries with the computers! Please, with great care- learned all you can about computers. This modern days, one must speed up to catch up with the youths! If you are like me, it is sheer torture! The Lord has been my Greatest teacher! Asked! Asked! Prayed and Never Give Up! Well, perhaps you might remember seeing me around. I'm sured that some, certainly noticed me, in all this aggravation! Please, I am so deeply thankful for All Beloved that has helped me through this. Readers, when you are reading, remembered that you are a most significant part of my life. May the Lord blesses your heart with joy. Amen.

*It is true that all things is Possible with God! Faith in God! Upon a close analization of the pattern of my life, I am completely humbled to God for the workings of his miraculous wonders; every details and occurrences have establishes an astoundingly solid purpose of joy. Tis of great blessings to undergo the changes of my life! There is no regrets because everything comes into focus, to let me understand how I was, the person I am today and yet further more, deep Revelations of God; Eternal Love of Grace and Mercy. Every Soul is so greatly blessed with the Attributes of God! Hallelujah! Trust in God wholeheartedly, much trials and testings is taking you to another level. Is there not a connection? Those of us who live to see our grandchildren, will certainly see the many changes taking place. The Lord disciplined those he loves. Sometimes one cannot understand why things be the way they are, but it must be so for refining and purification.

In uncertain times, keep Faith, Beloved Ones. Though you may be tested and suffered beyond measures; the joy of The Lord will comforted you, always keep in mind that you are Priests for God Forever. I prayed daily for you; together, may we give Honor and Glory to God.

Job1:9"Does Job fear God for nothing?" Satan replied.10"Have you not put a hedge around him and his household and everything he has? You have blessed the works of his hands, so that his flocks and herds are spread throughout the land.11But stretch out your hand and strike everything he has, and he will surely curse you to your face."

12The Lord said to Satan, "very well, then, everything he has is in your hands, but on the man himself do not lay a finger."

The Lord is in Full Control of our lives; nothing can be done without his permission. Great is the example of Job's character, devotion to God through trials, afflictions and physical deterioration. Faith is so examplified, outreaching to the creations in thorough foresight, knowledge and consideration!

*Quite some years had gone by, and Praise God that I am still here breathing, living and am seeking the Lord Daily. At one point in my life, I was so greatly impacted by a most uniquely beautiful, master minded, destructive child. She came completely humbled, features pleasing to the eyes; looks like my own biological daughter. I was privileged to care for her; yet, not realizing that she had been to six homes already. Kalee, four years old, was a most intellectual child, always observant of people, surroundings. She took meds, seen many psychologists. Because having nurtured three of my own challenging children, my compassion for her was great. Much unpredictable, disruptive behaviors. The mind of the child is always studying you as well as you are studying her; out witting you in schemes for attention. Great are her thoughts changing so fast, repetitious timeouts is not the solution. Kalee's writings at certain moments reminds me like the weather forecast bars detecting the storms, earthquakes, ups and downs continuously. The child is so intellectually gifted as to manipulate, win you over with soft openly gestures, touching, getting on a stranger's lap, grabbing hands, huggings.

Upon many days taken Kalee to church; great was interruptions-running throughout the classrooms, pushing at me consistently; openly displays of intensive jealousy of my interactions with others, constant screaming, crying, tearing paper into tiny pieces. I remembered upon meeting Kalee for the first time, a very sweet, quiet child, seem lacking love and attention; obedient to every commands throughout visitations. But as time progresses, disobedient in alarming Demonic Possession, reminding me of the movie Omen. Though meds were given to calmed her, the Spirit within her knows exactly what she is doing. Praise the Lord that one day, taking her to another psychologist, great was the observations and evaluations that Kalee inflicted self as well as blames others.

Heartbreaking as it is, Kalee needed to be institutionalized. Deeply, I prayed always and Trusted in The Lord, for great is his wisdom and purposes in all things. Tis a most valuable lesson of Self-Control as well as the Mind is a Battlefield. Praise you O Lord, for you are my strength in Thanksgiving. Amen.

Life is of magnitudes rise and falls; yet Hope is Strength, for the Lord blesses those he loves.

Today, my husband, Joseph, Traumatic Brain Injury, together shared in Faith of Comfort that only God could give. Though trying as it is, the Lord had prepared me for his Great Purposes. Finding myself in the lives of many to encourages, strengthened Souls according to the Will of God. I greatly in Thanksgiving to God for Mercy, us both; because no one has cared so much for us in every need and concerns. Together we humbly worshipped the Lord daily, seeking God; sharing the Gospel- Healing, Forgiveness, Restoration! Everything is possible with God! (***Matthew 19:12)

Psalm25:8Good and upright is the Lord; therefore he instructs sinners in his ways. 9He guides the humble in what is right and teaches them his way.

Psalm139:13For you created my inmost being; you knit me together in my mother's womb.14I Praise you because I am fearfully and wonderfully made; your works are wonderful, I know that full well.15My frame was not hidden from you when I was made in the secret place. When I was woven together in the depths of the earth,16your eyes saw my unformed body. All the days ordained for me were written in your book before one of them came to be.

John16:13But when he, the Spirit of truth, comes, he will guide you into all truth. He will not speak on his own; he will speak only what he hears, and he will tell you what is yet to come.14He will bring glory to me by taking from what is mine and making it known to you.15All that belongs to the father is mine. That is why I said the spirit will take from what is mine and make it known to you.

Therefore; Beloved, Grace, Full of Mercy and Generosity abounding in Love, so gloriously, richly, Divinely given to All by the One and

Only God. I encourage you who are wearied, troubled, conflicting guilts, fears, iniquities; your freewill willingly surrendered all to the Hope of glory which unveiled your Soul to be purified to all Truths. Nothing can hold you down, for Victory is Strength of Righteousness!

Sins is separation from God! If your sins is public, Confesses it before the church! Repentance is resisting Satan! The truth will set you free! Your faith is in God, not mankind! The creations are all the parts coming together as One Body, Church, Christ, God-Lord of all.

Ephesians5:24Now as the church submits to Christ, so also wives should submit to their husbands in everything.25Husbands,love your wives, just as Christ loved the church and gave himself up for her26to make her Holy, cleansing her by the washing with the water through the word,27and to present her to himself as a radiant church, without stain or wrinkle or any other blemish, but Holy and blameless.

1Corin.3:16Don't you know that you yourselves are God's temple and that God's Spirit lives in you?

God is perfection, Holy in all things. Confidence so richly embedded within all Souls; manifested of the workings of the Holy Spirit through Baptismal in joyous, faithful triumphant, prevailing all fears and evil in victory!

Furthermore, the significant relationship One has with God must be of integrity, genuiness. In order to be at Peace, all Confessions be dealt with, that is acceptance of sins, consequences, disciplined. Humble yourself before the Lord. Prayed, fear God, do right! Generosity of your heart towards mankind. Quit habits leading to death!

Stop sinning! Tis not as hard as you may think, because God is there. It is not shameful, but a humility which shall be conquered in healing, no longer this weight that has prisoned you in deadly grief, but set free, delivered in deep love, respect. There is not one Soul that do not sin, so do your best and God will do the rest! Thanksgiving to the Lord for all that he has done for you, asked for mercy, forgiveness; for the Lord is just and may pardons you. The Lord is Faithful because he is the One and Only Marvelous, Magnificent Father of all. Amen.

PATIENCE AND SELF-CONTROL

Much trials and testings have come so that your faith increases in genuiness, sure, solid. One must tests all Spirits, be disciplined; In time, days, weeks, months, years till

joyous of Confidence achieved in singing. Having success, prosperity, championships is focusing on the positive only; pushing forward towards goals, aim high, good deeds, good fruits-generosity in giving. Avoid all negativity which hindered progress. The gentleness, kindness of humility will prospered with each passing day.

Walk in the Spirit of God, speak what you know! Lift up Souls! Your attitudes and generosity has a lot to do with who you are! Look out for the needs of others. Money has no value, but the love in action gives joy. If you extend love, consideration, integrity; the rewards is of blessings. "A Happy wife is a Happy husband". Building a house has a firm, sure foundation, so much more so is holiness-spiritually excellent union of husband and wife; One Body in Christ. True beauty and binding is strong in prayers, faith, commitment, encouragement daily as a solid rock of deep love and respect.

Brokenness, failures is a great lesson to be learned; yet, mercifully healed through the heart of God-Baptismal of the Body of Christ-water and the Spirit in all Faithfulness of Obedience. Mindful that the judgement and wrath of God is absolutely fearful of condemnations; yet rejoicing in Peace of Rest.

PROSPERITY

Prayed, never give up! The Lord Jesus came in the physical so that Souls would be of Complete Oneness with God.

Hebrews9:27Just as man is destined to die once, and after that to face judgement,28so Christ was sacrificed once to take away the sins of many people; and he will appear a second time, not to bear sin, but to bring salvation to those who are waiting for him.

Proverbs 21:21He who pursues righteousness and love finds life, prosperity and honor.

A willing, humbled heart that is obedient to the teachings of God, will prospered in the ways and thoughts of God; making sound decisions, overcoming the physical-self, refined to Duty, spiritually serving God with all Heart and Soul.

When problems arises, plead your case before God. Prayed daily, the Lord is just and will blesses you based upon your conduct. Integrity and Righteousness is your faithfulness, shining Light of Joy! Acceptance in obedience to holiness. Give generously, wholeheartedly to All. Yet, Even though you may suffered injustices for doing good, Keep Faith, for the Lord may blesses you with greater joy.

In dangerous times, fear not, stand firm, if the Lord is willing, Armies of Righteousness is on the reserves to frustrates; gone ahead to annihilate the battles for you.

PEACE

*1Thes.4:11 Make it your ambition to lead a quiet life, to mind your own business and to work with your hands, just as we told you,12so that your daily life may win the respect of outsiders and so that you will not be dependent on anybody.

Tis a most powerful teachings of the Lord. Life would be absolutely endurable. the directions and instructions of the Lord rewards in blessings of joy, leading in comforts, path of Righteousness. Even though troubles may come, changes is taking place; set your eyes on Jesus, the Beloved Son of God. Be disciplined, morally and spiritually of excellenced, reverenced to God through the workings of the Holy Spirit.

A willing heart, devoted trustingly in all humility is an exquisite virtuous child, pleasing to God. Amen.

ROBBING GOD

Malachi 3:8"Will a man rob God? Yet you rob me. "But you ask, 'How do we rob you? "In tithes and offerings. 9You are under a curse—the whole nation of you—because you are robbing me. 10Bring the whole tithe into the storehouse, that there may be food in my house. Test me in this, "says the Lord Almighty, "and see if I will not throw open the floodgates of heaven and pour out so much blessing that you will not have room enough for it. 11 I will prevent pests from devouring your crops, and the vines in your fields will not cast their fruit, "says the Lord Almighty.

Generosity of Heart is Unlimited Action of Mind, Heart and Soul; an unconditional giving that fulfilled the Complete Spirit of God. Amen.

Thanksgiving to the Lord for the perfection of all created things-before the world began-Heaven and Earth, New Jerusalem! All life forms embracing in the acknowledgement of joyful reverence to Almighty God.

Hallelujah! What unison embodiment of Blessed confidence! Every Spirit is connected for purification, equal shares as rightful heirs of righteousness in the Kingdom of God; magnificently building up through the guidance and instruction of the Holy Spirit, manifested through Jesus-Death, Burial and Resurrection.

Therefore, the <u>Devotion of Giving to the Lord's House is an Expression of Deep Love, Respect, Sincerity</u>; what one has, not what one does not have. Yet even, can one gives All? Questioning not, freely given is much pleasing in the sight of God; for miraculous wonders of Blessings showers a joyful heart. Amen.

Should One dishonored and shamed The Lord for All that is given to mankind? Do your Duty with great joy and supplication! A house that is built up in unification as One Body, One God, One Church, One Faith, One Baptism is a spiritual body of life giving; stands firm, overcoming all things by the Providence of God.

As a child, carefree of innocence to the world; how satisfied seeking love, warmth, comforts. In my youth, the curiosity increases of explorations, expansion for a sense of who am I; what is life? Upon marriage and children-trials, tribulations, challenges. Through the brokenness, prayers, will of Confessions before the Lord in wholeheartedness; thanksgiving to the Lord for the privilege of understanding, knowledge in all Humility of the Mercy, Compassion, Grace and Peace. Joy lifted my mind, strength, body, Heart and Soul to love, and forgive unconditionally; seeing that together, Souls are completely refined in the Purity Eternal Enlightenment of God. Praise, Glory, Honor, Thanksgiving to God, in Jesus Name, Amen.

*CONFIDENCE IN GOD

Psalm 37:3Trust in the Lord and do good; dwell in the land and enjoy safe pasture. 4Delight yourself in the Lord and he will give you the desires of your heart.

And how True are the Words of the Lord; forever giving life, sustainment, blessings Souls to the Eternal Kingdom of God! All creations are all the parts coming together as One Body of Christ, created spiritually in such uniqueness of quality, character, hearts of purpose. The path of righteousness so ever present, leading Souls towards the Road to Redemption, prosperity(Prov.8:1-36).

Magnificently, a privilege, willingness of joyful acceptance commitment of total self to God.

Judges 9:56Thus God repay the wickedness that Abimelech had done to his father by murdering his seventy brothers. 57God also made the men of Shechem pay for all their wickedness. The curse of Jotham son of Jerub-Baal came on them(Judges 9:22-57).

Because Abimelech took action into his own hands for vengeance for what he thought was justified, great was his downfall as well as those who conspired with him. One must be so careful in the desires of the heart. Do what is good, fairness and of justice; above all, obedience to the authority. The compromising to Evil will results in Retribution of God. The Depth and Soul of our Heart must be in all Humility to do right. Inquired of God; prayers and petitions to the Lord with great respect. Integrity of heart may be heard for healing; blessings is granted if the Lord is willing.

By trusting wholeheartedly, disciplined through the teachings of the Lord; the rewards is immeasurable! The joy of the Lord consumed your Soul completely in confidence to be productive and effective; making a difference, changes pleasing to God.

Love, Generosity of Heart, Self-Control, Forgiveness; All divinely manifested within inner self, through the Disciplined Providence of God.

Genesis 31:40This was my situation: the heat consumed me in the daytime and the cold at night, and sleep fled from my eyes. 41It was like this for the twenty years I was in your household. I worked for you fourteen years for your two daughters and six years for your flocks, and you changed my wages ten times. 42 If the God of my father, the God of Abraham and the fear of Isaac, had not been with me, you would surely have sent me away empty-handed. But God has seen my hardship and toil of my hands, and last night he rebuked you.

This powerful story of Jacob's life is a great example of discipline and restoration from sins; Evils workings, yet changing in Faith of Humility of Prosperity and Righteousness(Gen.27-Gen.35).

How magnificently and of Generosity is the Lord in making all things new in wisdom through Jesus-the Oil of Joy in Eternal Prosperity,

Love, Grace and Mercy. The Lord Jesus ministry of spiritual food, is to bring Glory to God, One and Only Holy Father God of All. Peace is within the Creations since the beginning of Eternity. Amen.

Life's journeys are changes, blessings, gloriously designed in unity formation, joyous duty, always faithful in crown of righteousness.

Honor and Thanksgiving to the Lord for Grace, Love and Mercy of compassion. How great is the Eternal Love of God-refining mankind to love with complete knowledge, understanding, wisdom of humility. Lord, my Heart and Soul sings praises to your Holy Name. Let Every Church, One body, One God; together prayed in unison to Almighty God, the Eternal King.

Amen

Hallelujah! We are One! Marvelously, Completely Healed through the Miraculous Wonders of God, fear not in worldly things, but confidently in the Eternal Hope of Righteousness.

2Chronicles 30:18Although most of the many people who came from Ephraim, Manasseh, Issachar and Zebulun had not purified themselves, yet they ate the Passover, contrary to what was written. But Hezekiah prayed for them, saying,

"may the Lord, who is good, pardon everyone 19who sets his heart on seeking God—the Lord, the God of his fathers—even if he is not clean according to the rules of the sanctuary" 20and the Lord heard Hezekiah and healed the people.

Tis gloriously of blessings for the Love of the Lord has always and Eternally been since Heaven and Earth, yet still throughout the ages, today and beyond Eternity. Thanksgiving and Honor in Reverence to our One and Only Almighty God, King of Righteousness! Prayers in Devotion to his Majesty; sing, sing, let every heart Praising God in joyful wholeheartedness! Amen! Amen! Amen!

Printed in the United States
By Bookmasters